FOREST PARK

A WALK THROUGH HISTORY

Carolyn Mueller

REEDY PRESS

Dedication

This book is dedicated to my husband, John Kelly.
We met, married, and have run miles and miles together in Forest Park.
Here's to many miles more.

Reedy Press
PO Box 5131
St. Louis, MO 63139
www.reedypress.com

Cover design: Jill Halpin
Cover images: *Top*–Randy Allen (www.rsaphoto.com). *Bottom*–Missouri History Museum.
Interior design: Claire Ford

Library of Congress Control Number: 2019936710

ISBN: 9781681062211

Printed in the United States
20 21 22 23 24 5 4 3 2 1

TABLE OF CONTENTS

FOREWORD

One of the most welcome and appreciated phrases in the English language is "a walk in the park." This idiom was popularized in the twentieth century and became a descriptive referring to something most agreeable, comforting, pleasant, delightful, and readily accomplished. According to language specialist Christine Ammer, the celebrated writer James Patterson used the idiom in his 2004 book, *London Bridges*, when one of his curious characters checks on the health of his grandmother—"Everything fine there. Walk in the park, right, Nana?"

Author Carolyn Mueller similarly reassures us that everything is fine in a place known as the "heart of St. Louis." That would be Forest Park, a colossus of lakes, hills, wetlands, woodlands, and endless recreational opportunities. Forest Park also is the premier setting for first-class museums of art, history, and science; the world-renowned Saint Louis Zoo; and an amazing outdoor theater that St. Louisans affectionately call the Muny. At almost 1,300 acres, Forest Park exceeds the size of New York's Central Park by one-third, with plenty of room for a balloon glow, Earth Day, Shakespeare in the Park performances, and much more. "Everything's fine in Forest Park, right, Nana?"

Expert guide and outdoor enthusiast Mueller shows us just how fine Forest Park is with not just one "walk in the park" but seven intriguing walking tours beginning with the Art Hill Walk and concluding with a perimeter tour she has dubbed the Six-Mile Outer Park Loop. Each one of her walking tours highlights numerous must-sees along the trail and provides background on what you are taking in as a hiker, jogger, or leisurely walker. In truth, just one of these wonderful sites would be more than enough

inspiration and justification for you to put on your walking shoes.

On her Art Hill Walk, Mueller takes time to tell you all about the architectural inspiration behind the magnificent Saint Louis Art Museum and then sends you for a look at the fountains of the Emerson Grand Basin. On the River Loop Walk, she offers you encounters with the enchanting Cabanne House, the Forest Park Hatchery, Round Lake, the memory-making Steinberg Skating Rink, and the ever-popular art deco Jewel Box greenhouse. On the Eastern Loop Walk, Mueller teases you to take a look up at the thirty-three-foot sculpture in front of the Planetarium entitled *Looking Up*. She also insists that you pause to ponder the enormous sculpture *Animals Always*, celebrating the Saint Louis Zoo, as well as the sprawling World's Fair Pavilion, which is a Spanish-style work of art in its own right.

I must admit that as a tree-hugging type of guy, I am partial to Mueller's Nature Walk at the back of the book. This nature excursion begins at Kennedy Forest, a woodland area cared for by Forest Park Forever's Nature Reserve staff in partnership with the Missouri Department of Conservation. The Nature Walk takes you through the pollinator refuge of the Savanna in Kennedy Forest and by the 1904 Flight Cage of the Saint Louis Zoo, which is home to more than twenty species of North American birds.

If life's travails call for a bridge over troubled waters, consider the walking tour that takes you over the Prairie Boardwalk north of the Steinberg Skating Rink. Or, consider a hike over the Victorian Footbridge, which has served as the entryway to Forest Park from the city's Central West End neighborhood. On the east side of Forest Park, just across Kingshighway, are the hospital complexes where the sick can be healed and lives are often saved. It's an easy walk from these hospitals to the many special places described in Mueller's *Forest Park: A Walk through History*.

I do declare that I have taken "some comfort there"—at those special places in Forest Park—when friends and relatives have been in crisis at the healthcare centers along Kingshighway. No promises, but I can attest from personal experience that walks in the park can help get you through life's difficulties. Let Carolyn Mueller be your guide.

—Prof. Don Corrigan
Environmental/Nature Journalism Program
Webster University School of Communications

INTRODUCTION

For more than 140 years, Forest Park has functioned as a proverbial playground for the citizens of St. Louis and its visitors. This green expanse of trees and pathways, hills and fields, and winding ribbons of water perched on the edge of the city has served as a site for recreation, education, and gatherings of all types—from a simple family picnic to the landmark 1904 Louisiana Purchase Exposition (also known as the St. Louis World's Fair). Generations of St. Louisans have hiked through the trails of Kennedy Forest or sledded down Art Hill. Many have marveled at a glowing field of hot air balloons, enjoyed Shakespeare under a starry sky, or stood in awe before the works of Monet. Runners flock together at dawn and dusk and fishermen perch like water birds on the edges of Jefferson Lake. Behind this bustling backdrop lurk the shadows of history—those who built and fought for the park and those who have cared for and renovated it over and over again through the years. It's a landscape touched by history, where memories of the 1904 World's Fair and the legacy it left behind are found in every corner. It's also a respite from busy city life, a place to hear birdsong, to walk through peaceful green paths, to refresh and recharge. Today, Forest Park plays host to more than thirteen million people each year.

Forest Park is home to cultural institutions and beautiful locales, fit for any leisurely excursion on any given day. And throughout the year the park plays host to performances, festivals, and events, serving as a backdrop for many St. Louis memories. Each summer, Shakespeare in the Park presents free, open-air performances. The Saint Louis Symphony Orchestra puts on a free concert at the bottom of Art Hill. The Great Forest Park Balloon Race, held intermittently in the 1970s and now an annual event, includes not just the race, but also the beloved evening Balloon Glow. In some years, Forest Park has been the backdrop for Fair St. Louis, the multiday Fourth of July celebration. Other big events include the St. Louis Earth Day Festival, Bark in the Park (for the Humane Society of Missouri), the St. Louis African Arts Festival, and a variety of running races, from the 5K Make Tracks through the Zoo to portions of the GO! St. Louis Marathon. As was intended by its founders, Forest Park is the perfect gathering ground for St. Louisans, making it an ideal event space.

Forest Park can be explored by many modes of transportation, but the best way to know its paths and treasures is on foot. On a walking tour, visitors are able to take the time to appreciate the park's historical markers and natural wonders, there for discovery.

This book can serve as a guide to the many facets of the park, from monuments and memorials to waterfowl and wildflowers. Enjoy the journey and be open to exploration as you venture into this crown jewel of St. Louis, our own Forest Park.

Why Forest Park?

St. Louis is lucky to have such a phenomenal park as part of the city. But how did Forest Park actually come to be? Following the Civil War, St. Louis city planners advocated for a large park. Many different factions of society had a stake in this plan. A significant park could become a tourist attraction and would help to improve property values in the region. The building and maintenance of the park would provide jobs for unemployed workers. And, of course, a park could provide a place for St. Louisans to recreate, relax, and enjoy the outdoors. Forest Park opened in 1876, more than a decade after it was first proposed. Quickly, the space was geared up to host the 1904 Louisiana Purchase Exposition, also known as the 1904 World's fair. The fair and the funds procured in its aftermath changed the face and shape of the park, defining it for decades and inspiring buildings, sculptures, and pathways. In the one-hundred-plus years since St. Louis hosted the fair, Forest Park has undergone a variety of renovations that have maintained the integrity of its original purpose—to serve as a place to host the city's visitors and as a location for everyone to congregate, recreate, relax, and have fun in a beautiful outdoor space.

Note: For the purposes of this book, a "walk" is designated as a path from one place to another whereas a "loop" returns you to your starting point.

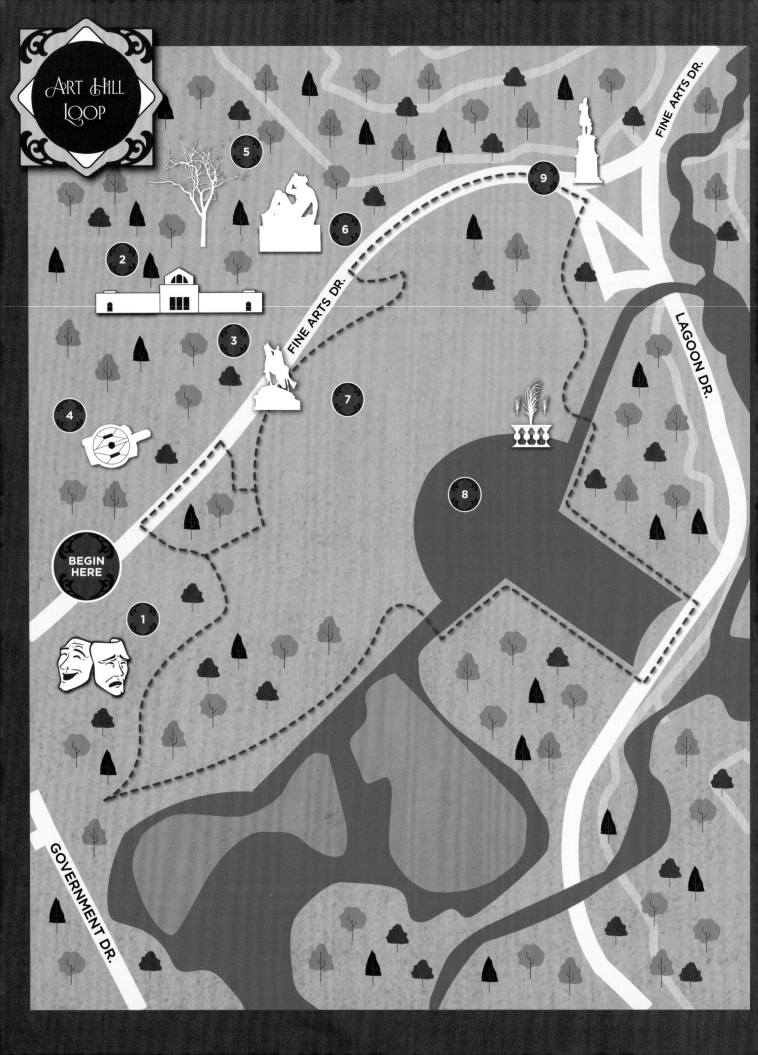

TOUR 1

Art Hill Loop
1.4 miles

👣 As you head north up Fine Arts Drive to the Saint Louis Art Museum, don't miss Shakespeare Glen on your right, on the east side of Art Hill.

❶ Shakespeare Glen

In 2001, St. Louis's first Shakespeare Festival opened in Forest Park, with *Romeo and Juliet* as the first show. Since its initial two-week run, Shakespeare Festival St. Louis has produced a free show each summer in the glen next to Art Hill. *A Midsummer Night's Dream* and *Romeo and Juliet* have been the two most common shows so far.

PHOTO BY DAVID LEVY

PHOTO BY STEVE JETT

❷ Saint Louis Art Museum

The Art Museum sits at the top of Art Hill. It was located downtown in the late nineteenth century but moved to its current location and building as part of the 1904 World's Fair. It is the only permanent building in Forest Park that was built for the World's Fair. Modeled after the Baths of Caracalla in Rome, it was designed by architect Cass Gilbert. The Saint Louis Art Museum is home to thirty thousand works of art including Egyptian mummies, several paintings by Monet and Van Gogh, early Native American art, and the world's largest collection by German painter Max Beckmann. Though some exhibitions include a fee, admission to the general museum is free every day. Admission to special exhibitions is free on Fridays.

👣 Be sure to spend some time with the art placed outside the museum. Begin with two works at the front of the building, one on the lawn and one just across Fine Arts Drive.

❸ *Apotheosis of St. Louis*

The *Apotheosis of St. Louis* is one of the most iconic sculptures in the city. This sculpture of the city's namesake, King Louis IX of France, is made of bronze and was donated by the Louisiana Purchase Exposition Company after the completion of the 1904 World's Fair. The statue is a bronze version of a plaster design made by artist Charles Henry Niehaus. The original plaster version stood at the entrance to the World's Fair (where the Missouri History Museum now stands). Niehaus offered to create a bronze version for $90,000. A local artist named W. R. Hodges bid $37,000, and the company chose him to create the sculpture. Niehaus sued and received $3,000, plus the insignia "designed by C. H. Niehaus" on the base of the statue, as a result. Now the statue sits proudly at the top of Art Hill, where it has represented the city of St. Louis since its unveiling in 1906.

PHOTO COURTESY OF THE
MISSOURI HISTORY MUSEUM

④ Giant Three-Way Plug, Scale A

The *Giant Three-Way Plug* is, pardon the pun, quite a shock to see sprawled out on the Saint Louis Art Museum's front lawn. This large plug is part of the museum's permanent collection and was created by American pop artist Claes Oldenburg.

PHOTO COURTESY OF FOREST PARK FOREVER

👣 **To see another outdoor sculpture, make your way to the lawn on the west side of the building (the right side if you're facing the museum's main entrance).**

⑤ Placebo

Placebo is planted on the western lawn of the Saint Louis Art Museum. A shiny, metal tree among living trees, *Placebo* was constructed out of twenty-four different stainless-steel pipes and rods. Its branches weigh more than five thousand pounds!

PHOTO BY LINDA BALLARD

👣 **On the south, or rear, side of the museum, you'll find more works of art and nature.**

⑥ Grace Taylor Broughton Sculpture Garden at the Saint Louis Art Museum

You don't have to go into the Saint Louis Art Museum to enjoy its works of art! The Sculpture Garden, where you can view modern and contemporary sculpture, incorporates landscape and art just outside the museum. The garden was designed by French landscape artist Michel Desvigne. Each "room" of the garden is segmented by over 450 hornbeam and serviceberry trees, creating a peaceful, Zen-like atmosphere for visitors.

👣 **When you're standing at the main entrance to the Saint Louis Art Museum, you're atop Art Hill. Look across Fine Arts Drive and behold the dramatic slope down to the Grand Basin, one of St. Louis's ideal spots for fun in all seasons!**

⑦ Art Hill

The massive expanse of Art Hill, which connects the Saint Louis Art Museum to the Emerson Grand Basin, is one of the most iconic locations in St. Louis. Congregating on Art Hill for a variety of activities is a tradition for many St. Louisans. Art Hill is the perfect spot to picnic, fly a kite, go sledding, see a summer outdoor movie, listen to the Saint Louis Symphony Orchestra, take photos, or exercise. Try running to the top!

PHOTO COURTESY OF THE MISSOURI HISTORY MUSEUM

As you stand at the top of Art Hill, you'll see two gently sloping paths—one to the left and one to the right—that arc around the sides of the hill to the Grand Basin. Or, if you're feeling frisky, just run headlong downhill (or take a sled if there's snow)!

8 Emerson Grand Basin

The Grand Basin was the center of the action during the 1904 World's Fair. During the fair, temporary "palaces" made from plaster and wood lined the sides of the basin for the entertainment of the fair's twenty million attendees. The Grand Basin was renovated in 2003, adding the eight lit fountains, and is named for Emerson Electric Company. Today it is a popular photo spot, as well as a quiet place to read, picnic, or exercise.

PHOTO BY STEPHEN SCHENKENBERG

Continue following the contours of the Grand Basin—whether you're on the left or right side—to the northeast, where the basin is bounded by Lagoon Drive. Across Lagoon is Lake Eisenhower.

After you've contemplated Lake Eisenhower, head to the west along Lagoon Drive or cross back to the Grand Basin side of Lagoon and take the winding walkway west along the golf course. Both the path and the road intersect with Fine Arts Drive. In the grassy triangle at the intersection stands the Edward Bates statue.

9 Edward Bates

The tribute to Edward Bates (now standing at the intersection of Fine Arts and Lagoon Drives) was the first statue ever erected in Forest Park. Edward Bates was United States attorney general under Abraham Lincoln from 1861 to 1864. Bates was born in Virginia in 1793 and moved to the St. Louis area in 1814, where he became a lawyer. He served in the Missouri House and Senate, as well as the US House of Representatives. This statue was originally meant for Lafayette Park, but it ended up being dedicated in Forest Park in 1876, along with the official park dedication.

PHOTO COURTESY OF FOREST PARK FOREVER

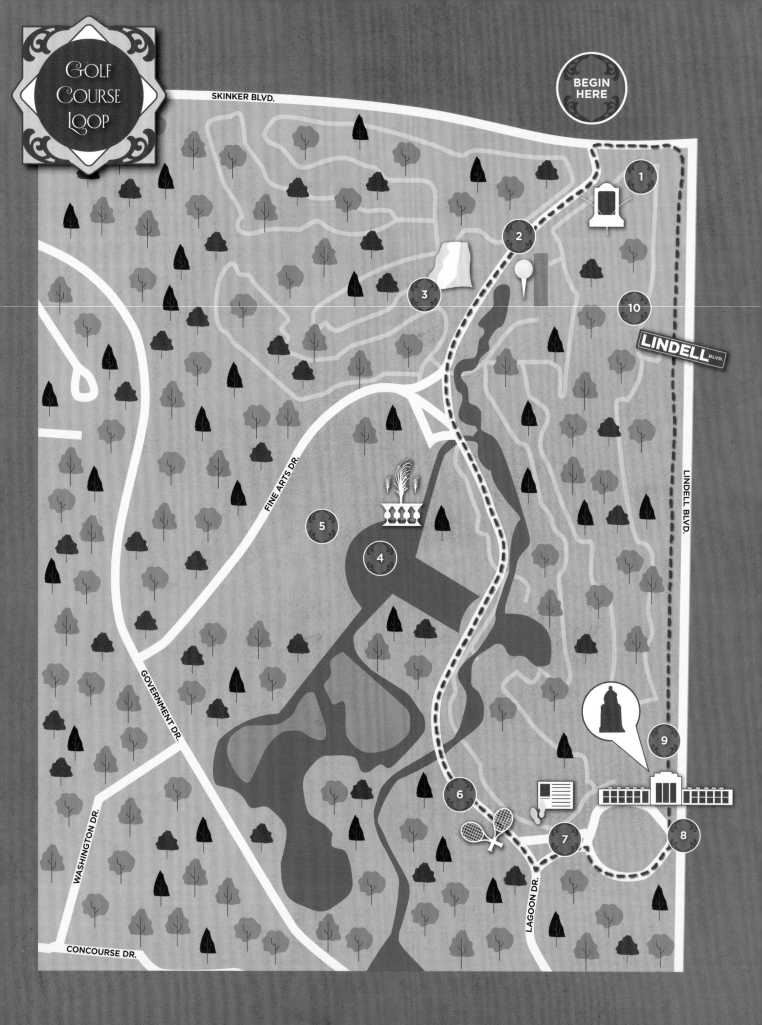

GOLF COURSE LOOP

Starting at Washington University or the Missouri History Museum, 2.1 miles

👣 The *Musicians Memorial* is located just east of the Lagoon Drive entrance to Forest Park, at the intersection of Lagoon and N. Skinker Boulevard. Walk east once you enter the park, and the memorial will be on your left.

① *Musicians Memorial*

The bronze relief on this sculpture portrays Pan, the Greek flute-playing god. The fountain in front was restored in the 1980s by radio station KMOX in memory of Jack Carney, a longtime morning show host. Need a drink? There are drinking fountains for park visitors in front of this memorial.

PHOTO COURTESY OF FOREST PARK FOREVER

👣 From the *Musicians Memorial*, continue southeast into the park along Lagoon Drive. You'll notice that you're walking through a golf course. If you want to visit the clubhouse or see the facilities (the course is open to the public), turn left into the entrance at 6141 Lagoon Drive.

② Norman K. Probstein Golf Course

The golf course in Forest Park has served as the setting for various championship golf events over the years, including the 1929 National Public Links Championship. Its three nine-hole courses are, fittingly, named after trees—Hawthorne, Dogwood, and Redbud.

PHOTO BY ANNE GROSSMANN

👣 Just past the entrance to the golf course is Flegel Falls (also known as the Cascades). Continue along Lagoon Drive to the southeast, and you'll see the falls on the right.

③ Flegel Falls

During the 1904 World's Fair, a waterfall called the Cascades ran down Art Hill near Festival Hall. In the 1930s, the Works Progress Administration built a seventy-five-foot waterfall west of Art Hill that was named Flegel Falls/the Cascades in honor of the original falls. The falls are the origin of the entire park's river system.

PHOTO BY STEVE JETT

👣 Once you've enjoyed the Cascades, continue your journey southeast along Lagoon Drive. You'll soon see a grassy triangle to your right in the center of Lagoon's intersection with Fine Arts Drive. Here stands the Edward Bates statue.

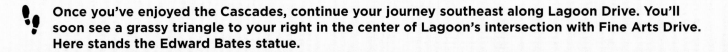

👣 Spend some time with Mr. Bates (see page 3), and then continue along Lagoon Drive, which turns slightly to the northeast. The body of water you'll soon see to your right is the Emerson Grand Basin. There is also a walking path that parallels Lagoon Drive to the basin—access it to the right, just past the intersection of Fine Arts Drive after you've crossed a small bridge.

④ Emerson Grand Basin

See page 3.

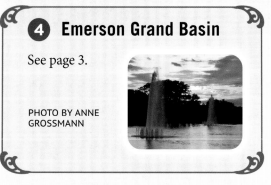

PHOTO BY ANNE GROSSMANN

👣 A small plaza opens onto the Grand Basin from Lagoon Drive. To the right and the left of the basin are paths that circle the water and lead to Art Hill.

⑤ Art Hill

See page 2.

PHOTO COURTESY OF THE MISSOURI HISTORY MUSEUM

👣 Continue your walk along Lagoon Drive, which turns northeast again, or use the walking path that parallels the road from the Grand Basin's plaza. After crossing a small bridge, you'll see Langenberg Field on the right. Walk past Langenberg Field—using the sidewalk or the walking path parallel to it—and you'll encounter the Dwight Davis Tennis Center on the right.

PHOTO COURTESY OF FOREST PARK FOREVER

DID YOU KNOW?

Langenberg Field hosts a variety of events, including sports games and practices and festivals.

⑥ Dwight Davis Tennis Center

PHOTO BY STEVE JETT

Dwight F. Davis was born in 1879 and became the director of parks in St. Louis in the early twentieth century. He also founded the Davis Cup, the most prominent international men's team event in tennis. As an advocate for outdoor recreation, he is responsible for removing all "Keep Off the Grass" signs from St. Louis city parks. He was also the secretary of war during the late 1920s. The Dwight Davis Tennis Center features eighteen lighted courts and a stadium court that seats up to 1,700 spectators. A few of the famous players who have competed here include Lindsay Davenport, Kim Clijsters, Pete Sampras, Venus and Serena Williams, Anna Kournikova, and Andy Roddick. Dwight Davis Tennis Center has many of the amenities of a private tennis club, but it is open for public use.

 As you walk past the tennis center, Lagoon Drive takes a sharp left turn. Take that left and follow Lagoon north until you intersect with DeBaliviere Circle. Directly in front of you is the Missouri History Museum.

7 Missouri History Museum

PHOTO BY STEVE JETT

The Missouri History Museum is the home of the Missouri Historical Society, which migrated from its former home downtown to the current building in Forest Park in the early twentieth century. Designed by Isaac Taylor, the Missouri History Museum was the first national monument to honor Thomas Jefferson and was built in 1913 on the site of the former entrance to the World's Fair. Here you can learn about the history of the St. Louis region, the World's Fair, the Lewis and Clark expedition, and Charles Lindbergh's historic transatlantic flight, as well as see rotating exhibitions on a variety of topics like civil rights, fashion, and baseball.

8 Thomas Jefferson

This statue of Thomas Jefferson was unveiled exactly nine years after the 1904 World's Fair, with businesses and schools closing for half a day so that St. Louisans could attend the ceremony. The statue was enclosed in its current location in 1985.

PHOTO COURTESY OF THE MISSOURI HISTORY MUSEUM

9 History Underfoot

To find these "sculptures," you just need to look under your feet! History Underfoot consists of twenty-two engraved bronze plates embedded in Missouri red granite blocks sunken into the sidewalks that surround the Missouri History Museum, the Dwight Davis Tennis Center, and the Dennis & Judith Jones Visitor and Education Center. The blocks detail interesting tidbits of St. Louis history and provide park visitors with an educational opportunity while they explore the park. They were installed during the parking lot renovations in 1998–99.

PHOTO COURTESY OF
FOREST PARK FOREVER

 Forest Park's northern boundary is Lindell Boulevard. Access it from the main entrance of the Missouri History Museum.

10 Lindell Boulevard

Lindell Boulevard is one of the best spots in St. Louis for real estate spotting. This street, which borders the park's northern edge, is home to many of the finest homes in the region. These mansions were built by wealthy St. Louisans as part of the one-hundred-acre Catlin Tract between Skinker and DeBaliviere, a development started in 1909.

PHOTO COURTESY OF THE MISSOURI HISTORY MUSEUM

PICNIC
WALK

FINE ARTS DR.

LAGOON DR.

GOVERNMENT DR.

CONCOURSE DR.

BEGIN
HERE

1

5

2

3

4

TOUR 3

PICNIC WALK

Starting at the World's Fair Pavilion, 1.5 miles one way

Start your walk at the intersection of Government Drive and Washington Drive. Head northwest on the gravel pathway toward the Emerson Grand Basin.

1 Friedrich Jahn Memorial

You can't miss the Friedrich Jahn Memorial on your left. At forty-one feet long, this memorial stretches across the grassy space, honoring German gymnastics educator and nationalist Friedrich Jahn. Jahn founded the Turnverein, an international gymnastic and social society, in 1811. The memorial highlights a young man with a shot put on one side of Jahn's bust and a young female wand dancer on the other. The statue was funded by the North American Turn Bund, a German cultural society, in 1913. At that time, about 15 percent of the city of St. Louis was German, and many German cultural societies were popular. The memorial was restored by the American Turners in 1972, 1989, and 2013–14.

PHOTO COURTESY OF FOREST PARK FOREVER

Continue along the gravel path to the north and you'll reach the Emerson Grand Basin (see page 3).

PHOTO BY STEVE JETT

The Grand Basin lies at the foot of Art Hill.

PHOTO COURTESY OF FOREST PARK FOREVER

Several paths meander to the left and right up the hill, or just head straight up! Just before you cross Fine Arts Drive, you'll see a magnificent sculpture, *Apotheosis of St. Louis* (see page 1).

PHOTO BY KATY PEACE

Make your way back to the Grand Basin at the bottom of Art Hill. Instead of taking the gravel walkway to the right (the direction you came from), walk straight ahead across a gently arching bridge. Just over the bridge, you'll come to a T intersection—turn right (or turn left for a circular tour of this lovely little park). You'll soon see another walkway and a bridge to the right. Cross this bridge to reach St. Louisans' favorite picnic spot!

② Bridge to Picnic Island

Picnic Island, centrally located near the base of Art Hill/Emerson Grand Basin, is the perfect spot to spread out a blanket and plan a picnic by the waterways of Post-Dispatch Lake. The suspension bridge is a prime photo spot for many photographers in the park.

PHOTO BY KATY PEACE

👣 **Picnic Island is surrounded by the tributaries off Post-Dispatch Lake.**

③ Post-Dispatch Lake

In 1894, the *St. Louis Post-Dispatch* held a fundraising campaign for this beautiful waterway, so the lake was named in its honor. Post-Dispatch Lake is where St. Louisans come to play on the water. Most of the lake is shallow (around six feet), but some of it can be as deep as twenty feet. It is a great habitat for fish as well as water birds.

PHOTO COURTESY OF THE MISSOURI HISTORY MUSEUM

👣 **If you want to get out on the water (yes!), you'll need to get to the Boathouse. To get there from Picnic Island, follow any of the gravel trails generally to the east until you reach the suspension bridge. After you cross the bridge, turn right. The path will wind around to the historic Boathouse.**

④ The Boathouse

The Boathouse on Post-Dispatch Lake has been in its current location since 1894. Today, the Boathouse has evolved to include a delicious restaurant where diners can eat beside the water before or after adventuring out on paddleboats, stand-up paddleboards, canoes, or kayaks for rent.

PHOTO BY STEVE JETT

5 Wildlife Island

Wildlife Island lies within Post-Dispatch Lake. This island can only be accessed by boat, so lots of native plants and wildlife species—including birds, insects, and even eastern spiny softshell turtles—make their homes there. You can easily see the island from the walking path at the base of Art Hill or when renting a boat or paddleboard from the nearby Boathouse.

PHOTO COURTESY OF FOREST PARK FOREVER

If you want to connect your picnic walk to the River Loop Walk, exit the Boathouse and look for the gravel walkway to the left, heading northwest. This path soon comes to a T intersection; turn right and go east. Soon you'll come to another junction and you'll see a small bridge to your left. Cross the bridge and head northeast. At the fork, take the path to the left and you'll see the tennis center on your left. If you want to play a match (the center is open to the public), stay on the path until you reach Grand Drive. Cross Grand at the crosswalk and you'll see the Dennis & Judith Jones Visitor and Education Center just ahead.

TOUR 4

RIVER LOOP

Starting at the Dennis & Judith Jones Visitor and Education Center, 3.1 miles

1 Dennis & Judith Jones Visitor and Education Center

This building was originally built in 1892 as the Lindell Pavilion Streetcar Center. Today it serves as a central hub in the park. Forest Park Forever staff offices are here, as well as locker rooms for parkgoers, a banquet facility for rental, park information for visitors, and even a café. It is a common meeting place for running groups, birders, and others active in the park. And it serves as one of Explore St. Louis's five visitor information centers found throughout the St. Louis area.

PHOTO BY DON KORTE

 To reach Lindell Field, return to Grand Drive and turn left, walking east to Cricket Drive. Turn left on Cricket and you'll see Lindell Field on the left. For a less-trafficked route, exit the Visitor and Education Center at the rear and take the gravel trail to the right. This takes you directly to the field and intersects with Cricket Drive.

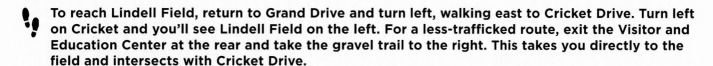 From Cricket Drive, take the second walkway to the right. If you've been walking on the gravel path already, just continue straight across Cricket. You'll soon see a very long, intimidating copper-green cannon on your right.

PHOTO COURTESY OF FOREST PARK FOREVER

2 Examinador, or the Spanish Cannon

This Spanish Cannon was forged in 1783 but did not show up in Forest Park until 1901. Despite the cannon residing in its current location along Lindell Boulevard for over a century, the story of its origins did not come to light until 2010, when a Forest Park Forever volunteer, Fred Ruhrwien, took it upon himself to research the history of the cannon. "Big Fred," as he is known around the park, learned that the cannon was turned over to the United States following the Spanish-American War in the late nineteenth century and given to St. Louis by the War Department in early 1900. Due to a lack of funding for the construction of a display, the cannon was stored in the St. Louis Mounted Police horse stables until a satirical article in the *St. Louis Post-Dispatch* written in the "voice" of the cannon chronicled the cannon's distress at living its life in a horse barn. Following the article, the cannon was installed in its current location in early 1901. Its name—Examinador—means "the Inspector."

PHOTO BY DON KORTE

From the Examinador, continue east on the gravel walkway until you reach Union Drive. Turn left on Union and just ahead on the left is your next destination, a first in the West!

❸ Cabanne House

The Cabanne House was built by Jean Pierre Cabanne in 1819 and was the first brick farmhouse built west of the Mississippi River. The current Cabanne House was reconstructed by St. Louis architect James H. McNamara in 1876, just in time for the opening of Forest Park. It reflects mid-Victorian architecture, and its rooms, featuring fourteen-foot ceilings and marble mantels, housed park superintendents and commissioners for years. It was renovated in 2006 and today is used as a rental facility.

PHOTO COURTESY OF FOREST PARK FOREVER

 Head back down Union Drive (the way you came to the Cabanne House). At the intersection with Grand Drive, you'll see two paths heading east to your left. The gravel path, which forks to the right, follows the contours of the water and is slightly longer. The paved path forks to the left and is more direct. Both paths come back together at—you guessed it!—Grand Drive. Turn left and you'll see the Forest Park Hatchery on the left.

❹ Forest Park Hatchery

The Forest Park Hatchery has a long history, dating back to 1879. With its original nine ponds, the hatchery was the first fish culture station in Missouri. It was at its largest in 1894, stocking 890,000 carp. In the late nineteenth century, aquarium railcars and milk cans were used to transport the fish. A small stone building, which remains today, was built near the hatchery to serve as the manager's office and living quarters. Today, the hatchery is not used to stock fish; instead, its five remaining ponds are used for educational programming through the Missouri Department of Conservation (MDC). Although fishing is permitted in Forest Park with a license, the hatchery ponds are only open through MDC programs. Anyone, however, can walk the trails around the hatchery and look for the many bird species that frequent the ponds.

PHOTO COURTESY OF FOREST PARK FOREVER

 From the Forest Park Hatchery, take Grand Drive back to the southwest. On your left is a round lake. (Guess what it's called?) Cross Grand at the crosswalk to take either the paved or gravel path along the south side of the lake.

❺ Round Lake

Round Lake is often recognized by its fountain, which was installed in 1916. With its quiet benches and lovely views of the neighboring willows, it is a favorite reading spot for many visitors.

PHOTO COURTESY OF FOREST PARK FOREVER

 Just past Round Lake, the gravel and paved paths merge. You'll see a stone and concrete bridge just ahead. Immediately after crossing this bridge, turn left onto a gravel path. Travel northeast along a wooded peninsula to find one of the park's special bridges.

6 Victorian Footbridge

The Victorian Footbridge was built in the late 1880s to provide easy park access from a nearby streetcar stop. The pony truss bridge, complete with Italianate ornamentation and fleurs-de-lis, provides an entryway to the park from St. Louis's Central West End neighborhood and is a popular and romantic photo spot.

Continue to the northeast to cross the Victorian Footbridge, and then turn immediately to the right onto a gravel path and wander generally south along a gravel path and boardwalk for some beautiful wetland scenery.

7 Prairie Boardwalk

This boardwalk runs through a beautiful wooded wetland and prairie just north of the Steinberg Skating Rink. It's a great place for taking photos, strolling, or birdwatching.

8 Prairie near Steinberg Skating Rink

As you walk along the Prairie Boardwalk, you'll be passing through a prairie near Steinberg Skating Rink. This former lawn and parking lot was restored to native prairie grasses and flowers beginning around the year 2000. Parkgoers can spot wildlife and observe the wetlands from boardwalks that run through the prairie. A diverse array of animals can be found here, including, but not limited to, purple martins, mink, bats, turtles, dragonflies, and monarch butterflies.

As you come to the end of the Prairie Boardwalk, you'll see a sculpture directly ahead.

9 *Joie de Vivre*

Joie de Vivre, which translates to "joy of living," is a lively sculpture created by Jacques Lipchitz in 1927, inspired by a serious illness suffered by his sister. The lightness and vivacity of the sculpture was meant to inspire her to hold onto life. The sculpture was donated by Etta E. Steinberg, who also donated the funds for the Steinberg Skating Rink, making the rink the sculpture's permanent home.

PHOTO BY LINDA BALLARD

As you pass the sculpture, you'll see a line of chess tables straight ahead. Sit for a game or two!

⑩ Chess Tables

The Saint Louis Chess Club and Scholastic Center of Saint Louis donated the chess tables that are located just north of Steinberg Skating Rink. Avid chess fans of all ages are welcome to gather here for a game year-round.

PHOTO COURTESY OF FOREST PARK FOREVER

 Continue walking straight ahead to lace on a pair of skates (but only in the winter!).

PHOTO BY BENJAMIN SHERLISS

⑪ Steinberg Skating Rink

Etta E. Steinberg, the widow of St. Louis investment banker Mark C. Steinberg, admired the outdoor skating rink in New York City's Central Park and dreamed of a similar venue for Forest Park. A donation was made from the Steinberg Charitable Trust to make her dream a reality. Steinberg is the Midwest's largest outdoor skating rink. It has been open since 1957 and has used real ice from the very first day—meaning that you cannot skate there past late February, when the ice melts. However, it is never too cold to skate at Steinberg, as they don't have a winter temperature cut-off. On the rink's opening day, a crowd of 2,500 people came out to skate! Today they offer ice-skating lessons, family hours, and even moonlight skating sessions.

 After skating (or dreaming of skating, depending on the season), return to the chess tables and follow the concrete path to the left. You'll quickly turn northeast and cross a small stone and concrete bridge. Immediately after crossing the bridge, take the left fork and cross Jefferson Drive (also called Faulkner Drive south of the walkway) at the crosswalk. The path will continue briefly along Wells Drive before turning north, and you'll crest a small hill. In front of you lies the Emerson Central Fields.

⑫ Emerson Central Fields

In 2019, Central Fields were renovated and formally christened Emerson Central Fields. This thirty-acre area of the park hosts a variety of events from soccer and rugby to cross country championships and the Great Forest Park Balloon Race.

PHOTO BY JENNIFER KORMAN

 As you walk along the perimeter of the Emerson Central Fields, look to your left and you'll notice the Highlands Golf & Tennis Center.

16   TOUR 4: RIVER LOOP

⓵③ Highlands Golf & Tennis Center

PHOTO BY STEVE JETT

The Highlands includes a nine-hole, 2,656-yard course. The Highlands Golf & Tennis Center has been in its current location since 1902, when the St. Louis Amateur Athletic Association (Triple A) was given seventy acres of land in the park. This area, once called Tierny Hill, was home to many athletic facilities, including tennis courts, a baseball diamond, a track, a golf course, handball and volleyball courts, and a lacrosse team, which went on to win the silver medal in the 1904 Olympics. The Triple A facilities hosted the Davis Cup in 1927, 1946, and 1961. Today, the Highlands boasts the city of St. Louis's only public clay tennis courts and driving range.

👣 **Continue straight past the concession stand, cross Wells Drive (also called Macklind Drive northwest of the intersection). Continue walking along Wells Drive and you'll be able to see more of the Highlands Golf Course to your left. You'll see an earthen-red sidewalk to the right that heads into an open greenspace. You can't miss your next destination, a spectacular architectural gem.**

⓵④ The Jewel Box

The art deco Jewel Box, opened in 1936, is an extraordinary greenhouse designed by William C. Becker. The structure is made from glass supported by arched steel beams to protect it from hail storms. When a storm broke a thousand panes of glass in the other Forest Park greenhouses in 1938, the Jewel Box remained intact. The greenhouse was renovated in 2002 and today is a popular St. Louis wedding venue. The Flora Conservancy of Forest Park works to maintain the plant life around the Jewel Box.

PHOTO COURTESY OF FOREST PARK FOREVER

👣 **After you've been through the aptly named Jewel Box, walk through the grassy area behind and to the right of the greenhouse. Directly behind the Colonial Daughter Fountain is a quiet but important memorial.**

⓵⑤ Korean War Memorial

PHOTO COURTESY OF
FOREST PARK FOREVER

The original Korean War Memorial in Forest Park was actually dedicated during the war—on July 2, 1951. This monument was a large planting in the shape of a clock that included twenty-five thousand flowers, but over the decades it gradually deteriorated. The current memorial was erected in 1989 in the shape of a working sun dial, keeping the original monument's representation of the passage of time. The sun dial includes the inscription *Diem Adimere Aegritudinem Hominibus*, or Time Heals All Wounds. The monument was designed by Marianist monk Brother Mel Meyer, who grew up just outside of St. Louis. Later additions to the memorial, including four granite benches to represent each chapter of the Missouri Korean War Veterans Association and two black granite tablets inscribed with the names of the 258 men and women from the area who died in the conflict, were added on the fiftieth anniversary of the armistice.

Walk around or through the stand of trees to the right of the Korean War Memorial to see a remnant of grand old St. Louis.

16 Vandeventer Place Gates

These granite and iron gates once marked the entrance to one of the most exclusive neighborhoods in St. Louis—Vandeventer Place. This neighborhood was founded in 1870 and named for Peter Vandeventer, a wealthy stockbroker who owned much of the land where it was built. Vandeventer Place was designed by Julius Pitzman, who later became the chief engineer for the development of Forest Park. The stately gates were installed in 1894. In 1947, the Veterans Administration demolished the eastern half of the neighborhood to build a new hospital, and shortly after the city tore down the western half to build a juvenile detention center. The gates were moved to Forest Park, and they're now all that remains of this once fashionable neighborhood.

PHOTO COURTESY OF FOREST PARK FOREVER

PHOTO BY DON KORTE

17 St. Francis of Assisi

St. Francis of Assisi was born into a wealthy Italian family, but he surrendered his inherited wealth in order to live a life of poverty and prayer. Francis, the patron saint of animals, was known for his love of animals and peace. The statue of St. Francis is located near the Jewel Box, in a garden that attracts dragonflies, butterflies, and birds. The statue, sculpted by Carl Mose, was commissioned by Alice Martin Turner in memory of her husband, Harry Turner. One of the first automobile dealers in St. Louis, Turner also raced cars at Fairground Park. During his lifetime, he became acutely aware of the "diseases of life" and spoke out about the ways of the social elite in St. Louis, an attitude his wife thought reflected the teachings of St. Francis—inspiring the commission of this statue.

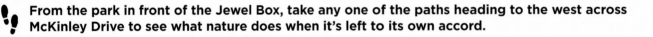 **From the park in front of the Jewel Box, take any one of the paths heading to the west across McKinley Drive to see what nature does when it's left to its own accord.**

18 Successional Forest

The Successional Forest area runs just west of the Jewel Box. This area was once simply turfed grass and landscaped trees and plantings. Thirty years ago, the forest here was left to grow and evolve on its own, offering visitors the chance to see a successional forest in the early stages of its development. These twenty-plus acres make for a peaceful place to run, walk, birdwatch, and enjoy the park's natural splendor.

PHOTO COURTESY OF FOREST PARK FOREVER

Wander north through the forest until you reach Concourse Drive, which runs between Carr Lane Drive and McKinley Drive. Cross Concourse to access a paved trail that heads north through a lovely wooded area. Although the trail has several forks and turns, no matter which you take, you'll end up at Government Drive just across from the parking lot for the Boathouse. Get ready for some fun on the water!

PHOTO COURTESY OF THE MISSOURI HISTORY MUSEUM

DID YOU KNOW?

The River des Peres used to flow through Forest Park, but around the turn of the twentieth century it became polluted and unsanitary due to citizens treating it like a sewer. As St. Louisans prepared to host the World's Fair in 1904, plans were made to hide the River des Peres from view. Using dynamite, a ditch was excavated creating an underground passageway for the river to flow through, out of sight of fairgoers. Today, this passageway is encased in massive concrete pipes beneath the park, and the River des Peres is now a National Historic Civil Engineering Landmark.

After you're done recreating on the lake and pondering the River des Peres, exit the front of the Boathouse and head north on the gravel path from the parking lot (away from Government Drive). When you come to a T intersection, turn right to the east. You'll soon come to another T—turn left onto a paved path and cross a small wood-plank bridge. Stay on this path and you'll see tennis courts on the left. You'll soon intersect with Grand Drive; turn left and follow Grand west to the tennis clubhouse, where you can book some *very* reasonable play.

To continue your walk on the Deer Lake Loop, head back to the east on Grand Drive. Just past the tennis courts, you'll see a crosswalk that takes you to the Dennis & Judith Jones Visitor and Education Center.

PHOTO BY DON KORTE

DEER LAKE LOOP

BEGIN HERE

GOVERNMENT DR.

GRAND DR.

MCKINLEY DR.

CRICKET DR.

CRICKET DR.

PAGODA CIR.

THEATRE DR.

GRAND DR.

SUMMIT DR.

UNION DR.

UNION DR.

FOREST PARK PKWY.

1
2
3
4
5
6
7
8
9

TOUR 5

DEER LAKE LOOP

Starting at the Dennis & Judith Jones Visitor and Education Center, 1.1 miles

1 **Dennis & Judith Jones Visitor and Education Center**

See page 13.

👣 To reach Lindell Field, return to Grand Drive and turn left, walking east to Cricket Drive. Turn left on Cricket and you'll see Lindell Field on the left. For a less-trafficked route, exit the Visitor and Education Center at the rear and take the gravel trail to the right. This takes you directly to the field and intersects with Cricket Drive.

👣 From Cricket Drive, take the second walkway to the right. If you've been walking on the gravel path already, just continue straight across Cricket. Stay on the gravel walkway until you reach Union Drive. Turn left on Union, and just ahead on the left is your next destination.

2 **Cabanne House**

See page 14.

👣 Your next stop is a statue of a patriot on horseback. Head back down Union Drive (the way you came to the Cabanne House). At the intersection with Grand Drive, you'll see the horseman directly across from you. Cross Grand at the crosswalk to check out this St. Louis hero.

PHOTO COURTESY OF THE MISSOURI HISTORY MUSEUM

3 **Franz Sigel**

This statue of German American general Franz Sigel was the first equestrian statue in St. Louis. It was sculpted by Robert Cauer as a way to honor Sigel and "remind future St. Louisans of the heroism of German-American patriots during the Civil War." Sigel immigrated to the United States in 1852 and lived in New York City until 1857, when he was hired to head the German-American Institute in St. Louis. Sigel became a leader of the pro-Unionist immigrant community when the Civil War broke out, and after the successful Battle at Pea Ridge in Arkansas, he was promoted to major general. After the war, he returned to New York, where he was active in politics and publishing. His monument was dedicated in 1906, four years after his death.

4 Savanna Ecosystems

Savannas are an important part of Missouri's native ecosystems. Missouri is a transition state between the forests in the east and the prairie in the west, and savannas incorporate both of these ecosystems, including grasslands full of wildflowers dotted with large trees like oaks. Essentially, savannas are prairies with trees, creating rich habitat for a variety of native wildlife species. Fire is critical to the health of savannas, helping to restore them annually. With this in mind, the savannas in Forest Park are maintained through prescribed burns. Forest Park is home to two main savannas—Deer Lake Savanna and the Savanna in Kennedy Forest. Deer Lake Savanna encompasses twenty-four acres. The Savanna in Kennedy Forest includes eight acres and is being restored in an effort that began in 1999. Both of these savannas are home to a rich biodiversity of plant and animal species that parkgoers will enjoy spotting.

 Behind the statue of Franz Sigel is a gravel path that will take you southwest into the Deer Lake Savanna. You'll see a small path to the left that leads to a stone circle.

5 Council Circle

This waterside circle sits in the Deer Lake Savanna. It is used by school groups and picnickers alike. It was completed in 2009.

PHOTO COURTESY OF FOREST PARK FOREVER

Rejoin the main path after you've visited Council Circle and continue southwest. This meandering trail will take you through the heart of the savanna to Deer Lake. As you approach the lake, you'll see the stones that create the riffles.

6 Deer Lake

Deer Lake is a prime picnic spot near the Muny. The Deer Lake Riffles offer a nice photo or wading location, while the aeration of the water improves the water quality in the park.

PHOTO COURTESY OF ONCE FILMS

7 The Muny

The Muny is the largest and oldest outdoor theater in the United States. It currently features Broadway-style musicals throughout the summer months. The Muny seats eleven thousand people, with 1,500 free seats reserved each night on a first-come, first-serve basis. The first performance at the Muny, on June 5, 1917, was *Aida*. The first show produced after the official founding and naming of the Muny in 1919 was *Robin Hood*. Some of the well-known stars who have performed on the Muny's renowned stage include Bob Hope, Cab Calloway, Yul Brynner, Gene Kelly, Debbie Reynolds, Richard Harris, Mitzi Gaynor, Phyllis Diller, Red Skelton, Cary Grant, John Travolta, Carol Burnett, Angela Lansbury, Ozzie Smith, Lauren Bacall, Bette Davis, W. C. Fields, Margaret Hamilton, Florence Henderson, Christopher Jackson, Davy Jones, Ethel Merman, Sarah Jessica Parker, Michelle Williams, Mickey Rooney, Betty White, and Phyllis Smith.

The lake across Pagoda Circle from the Muny is aptly named Pagoda Lake. In the center of the lake is a delightful bandstand.

8 Pagoda Circle/ Nathan Frank Bandstand

PHOTO COURTESY OF THE MISSOURI HISTORY MUSEUM

The original bandstand on Pagoda Lake was built in 1876 and then renovated for the 1904 World's Fair. Soon after, it was destroyed by a storm and fire. St. Louis lawyer Nathan Frank donated money for a renovation, which was completed in 1925. Frank's was the first private donation made to Forest Park. The last renovation done to this area was in 2000. The bandstand is built with white marble and concrete with bronze rails and a copper roof. Nathan Frank was vice president of the Louisiana Purchase Exposition (World's Fair) in 1904 and Missouri's first Jewish congressman.

From the entrance to the Muny, you can circumambulate Pagoda Circle (something folks might have done in 1876), or you can take the footpath cutting across the park just to the northeast side of the lake. When you reach the northeast side of the circle, you'll see a pitch perfect for cricket and rugby.

9 Cricket Field

Cricket Field hosts sports activities, particularly rugby. Ever wish you could go back in time and witness some 1860s-era baseball? Well, you can! Sort of. The St. Louis Cup, played on Cricket, Lindell, and Langenberg Fields in Forest Park showcases a competition between several area vintage baseball clubs, including the home team, the Saint Louis Brown Stockings. The matches are played with most of the existing rules for 1860s baseball, including vintage uniforms and even (sometimes) vintage mustaches to boot!

TOUR 6

EASTERN LOOP

Starting at the tunnel under I-64, opposite the entrance to the Saint Louis Science Center's Oakland Building, 4.3 miles

① Saint Louis Science Center

The Academy of Science of St. Louis was first founded in 1856—forming the roots of the Saint Louis Science Center. The Science Center began as the James S. McDonnell Planetarium in 1963. James Smith McDonnell, an aviation pioneer and cofounder of McDonnell Douglas (now Boeing), donated $200,000 toward the construction of the Planetarium, which was named in his honor. In 1985, it was rechristened the Saint Louis Science Center, and in 1991 the Oakland Building opened on the other side of I-64 as part of a $34 million expansion. It is now one of the largest science museums in the United States and includes a five-story, seventy-nine-foot domed OMNIMAX theater. The Science Center dedicates its exhibits to earth science, emerging technology, the life sciences, physical science, and chemistry.

PHOTO COURTESY OF
THE SAINT LOUIS SCIENCE CENTER

👣 Before you enter the Planetarium on the north side of the building, be sure to *look up* at the center of the drop-off circle.

② *Looking Up*

This sculpture of a figure looking up toward the sky is fittingly perched near the Planetarium. Designed by native St. Louisan sculptor Tom Friedman, it is thirty-three feet tall and made of stainless steel, along with crushed aluminum foil and other bits of distressed metal.

PHOTO COURTESY OF
THE SAINT LOUIS SCIENCE CENTER

👣 Hint: If you want to see the rest of the Science Center, follow the directions in the Planetarium to the skywalk crossing I-64/US 40, which will take you to the Science Center's Oakland Building, a can't-miss attraction.

DID YOU KNOW?

The Saint Louis Science Center Planetarium gets wrapped in a *giant* red bow every holiday season.

Just west of the James S. McDonnell Planetarium, across the parking lot (to the right, if you're facing the entrance), is a place to test your medieval (or modern) mettle.

③ Archery Range

The archery range is free and open for public use. On Sunday afternoons, anyone can join the St. Louis Archery Club for shooting practice. The club was founded in the 1920s and sponsored archery tournaments for young people here throughout the 1930s.

PHOTO COURTESY OF FOREST PARK FOREVER

At the southeast corner of the archery range is a bit of (ongoing) St. Louis history.

④ St. Louis Mounted Police Horse Stables

PHOTO COURTESY OF FOREST PARK FOREVER

The St. Louis Mounted Police horse stables were donated to the city of St. Louis in 1919 by the US Army. The building, once an old airplane hangar, was converted into stables and renovated in 2013. The Mounted Police patrol the park because they have access to places that a police vehicle might not. The horses, which usually donated to the police force, are geldings (castrated males) between five and ten years old. Currently, there are four police horses. St. Louis has a history of fits and starts with its Mounted Police program. In 1910, ten of the Mounted Police officers were unhorsed because of their weight. The program was then halted in 1948, as cars became commonplace, but it was revitalized in 1971, since the horses served an important and particular purpose for the park. In 1982, they proved their worth to the city by helping clear the crowds from downtown after the Cardinals won the World Series. Today, they are a fixture of Forest Park.

From the area of the archery range and the stables, several paths lead nearly due west around and through softball and baseball fields.

⑤ Boeing Aviation Field

From 1920 to 1921, this area was a landing field for airmail service between St. Louis and Chicago. At that time, the pilots were able to make the trip in approximately three and a half hours. Today, Boeing Aviation Field includes four baseball and four softball diamonds.

At the northwestern end of Aviation Field, you will run into McKinley Drive. Cross McKinley Drive and head west along the gravel path. To your left you should see the Department of Parks, Recreation, and Forestry complex. Continue forward and you will reach Hampton Avenue overpass (and walking tunnel). Before the tunnel, jump on the sidewalk that leads toward Hampton and enjoy the view of "Animals Always."

6 *Animals Always*

The southeastern corner of the Saint Louis Zoo is home to the remarkable *Animals Always* sculpture. At 130 feet long and 36 feet high, this is the largest sculpture at any public zoo in the United States. It includes more than fifty unique animal species, all of which can be found at the Saint Louis Zoo. This sculpture, designed by Albert Paley, took five years to create and weighs in at over 107 tons (that's the equivalent of twenty elephants!).

PHOTO COURTESY OF FOREST PARK FOREVER

 When you're done counting animals in the *Animals Always* sculpture, turn right on Concourse and head north, through the traffic circle at Washington Drive. Look to the right to check out the Nature Playscape.

7 Nature Playscape

Did you know that playing in and exploring nature is beneficial to almost all aspects of child development? With this in mind, Forest Park will create a Nature Playscape for kids of all ages to discover. Opening in 2020, the Nature Playscape will feature five distinct activity areas—a meadow, wetland, bottomland, spring, and mounds—connected by a series of paths and boardwalks. The Nature Playscape will not only be beneficial to children and families but also to the environment as it will turn what was once a turf grass field into a space for native and diverse plant species to flourish.

ARCHITECTURAL ILLUSTRATION © DESIGN DISTILL, COURTESY OF INTERBORO PARTNERS AND FOREST PARK FOREVER

Go on to the next traffic circle, where you'll see a stately pavilion to your left.

8 World's Fair Pavilion

The World's Fair Pavilion, built in a Spanish style, was finished in 1909 with funds from the 1904 World's Fair. The pavilion was renovated between 1998 and 2007 and is a popular spot for exercise, picnics, festivals, and special events.

PHOTO COURTESY OF THE MISSOURI HISTORY MUSEUM

Just outside the pavilion on the south side, you'll see a loving—and playful—memorial.

9 Turtle Monument at the World's Fair Pavilion

This turtle sculpture, nestled next to the grandeur of the World's Fair Pavilion, was designed by Bob Cassilly, the same man who created the Turtle Playground on the south side of the Tamm Bridge over I-64. *Turtle Monument* was created in memory of Myron Glassberg, a successful St. Louis contractor and patron of St. Louis parks. Myron's wife, Sonya "Sunny" Glassberg, funded the renovation of the World's Fair Pavilion as an eightieth birthday present to herself in 1998. Glassberg saw turtles as a representation of peace, so this sculpture was added as a surprise for her once renovations were complete.

PHOTO COURTESY OF FOREST PARK FOREVER

Once you've appreciated the memorial to Mr. Glassberg, walk through the pavilion to the north side. Ahead and down the hill, you'll see a fountain in a small basin. Head down the hill using the stairs or ramp. When you reach the pathway that runs in front of the fountain, turn left toward a small pine grove to see another monument to prominent St. Louisans.

10 *Pine* (the St. Louis Award Statue)

Pine is surrounded by a lovely grove of pine trees at the bottom of the hill below the World's Fair Pavilion. Sculptured by Kent Addison in 1965, *Pine* honors the recipients of the St. Louis Award, which honors "the resident of metropolitan St. Louis who, during the preceding year, has contributed the most outstanding service for its development." The award was established anonymously in 1931. In 1960, it was revealed that philanthropist David P. Wohl, founder of the Wohl Shoe Company, had created the honor. The sculpture is made from Cor-Ten steel, a naturally rusting material.

PHOTO COURTESY OF LINDA BALLARD

From *Pine*, take a right and follow the sidewalk in front of the fountain at the bottom of the World's Fair Pavilion (with the pavilion on your right) until you see a bike path emerge on the right-hand side (across the street from the Boathouse). Take the bike path as it meanders through the woods and opens up to the intersection of McKinley and Carr Lane Drive. Get your leg workout in by climbing the hill on Carr Lane Drive with the woods on your left.

⓫ Successional Forest

See page 18.

At the top of the hill, make a left on Wells Drive and continue to walk east. Just across from the first roundabout at Wells and McKinley, you'll discover a true architectural gem.

⓬ The Jewel Box

See page 17.

PHOTO COURTESY OF
FOREST PARK FOREVER

⓭ St. Francis of Assisi

See page 18.

PHOTO BY DON KORTE

Cross Wells at the roundabout and continue east, with Boeing Aviation Field on your right. If you look to the left, you'll see an expanse of green golf course. This is known as the Highlands Golf and Tennis Center.

⓮ The Highlands Golf and Tennis Center

The Highlands is a great place to recreate or host an event. It boasts a nine-hole golf course, a driving range, thirteen clay tennis courts, and event facilities. Or you can stop in for lunch at the restaurant, which features a patio overlooking the course.

PHOTO BY ISABEL ACEVEDO

Continue to wind along the path up the hill toward the Planetarium. You'll find the tunnel under I-64 on your right. You've completed the Eastern Loop Walk.

SKINKER BLVD.

GOVERNMENT DR.

INTERSTATE 64

WELLS DR.

TAMM AVE.

LAGOON DR.

LINDELL BLVD.

FINE ARTS DR.

WASHINGTON DR.

GOVERNMENT DR.

DEBALIVIERE CIR.

CONCOURSE DR.

CARR LANE DR.

GRAND DR.

PAGODA CIR.

MCKINLEY DR.

SUMMIT DR.

UNION DR.

THEATRE DR.

WELLS DR.

CLAYTON AVE.

WELLS DR.

JEFFERSON DR.

GRAND DR.

FAULKNER DR.

FOREST PARK PKWY.

W. PINE DR.

S. KINGSHIGHWAY BLVD.

SIX-MILE OUTER PARK LOOP

If you prefer to explore the park with wheels (or just want a long walk), the bike path encircling the outer edge is approximately six miles in length.

You'll see the following sites on this outer park loop. Feel free to access more information about each location using the index of this book.

1. Missouri History Museum
2. Thomas Jefferson
3. *History Underfoot*
4. Lindell Boulevard
5. Norman K. Probstein Golf Course
6. *Musicians Memorial*
7. Kennedy Forest
8. Saint Louis Zoo
9. Boeing Aviation Field
10. St. Louis Mounted Police Horse Stables
11. Archery Range
12. Saint Louis Science Center

13. Bowl Lake
14. Jefferson Lake
15. Steinberg Skating Rink
16. Chess Tables
17. *Joie de Vivre*
18. Prairie near Steinberg Skating Rink
19. Round Lake
20. Forest Park Hatchery
21. General Franz Sigel Statue
22. Cabanne House
23. Lindell Field
24. Dennis & Judith Jones Visitor and Education Center

BEGIN HERE

1

2

3

4

SKINKER BLVD.

WELLS DR.

GOVERNMENT DR.

WELLS DR.

OPTIONAL PATH

N 88

TAMM AVE.

GOVERNMENT DR.

FINE ARTS DR.

NATURE WALK
Beginning at the Skinker entrance, 1.4 miles

1 Kennedy Forest

Named in memory of President John F. Kennedy in 1964, Kennedy Forest was the first area of Forest Park to be dedicated to conservation efforts. It is a stopping point for over one hundred species of migratory birds and a home to many different frog species. Birders, runners, cyclists, and hikers frequent its three and a half miles of trails. The forest is cared for by Forest Park Forever's Nature Reserve staff in partnership with the Missouri Department of Conservation.

PHOTO COURTESY OF
FOREST PARK FOREVER

To reach the Savanna in Kennedy Forest, begin at the Skinker entrance to the park and take either the asphalt recreational path or the gravel recreational path north, paralleling Skinker Boulevard.

Savanna in Kennedy Forest

2 Savanna in Kennedy Forest was recreated in 1999 by a group of volunteers whose goal was to create a savanna habitat very close to that originally found in the St. Louis region. This eight-acre stretch of native plants is home to many bird species and a number of native pollinators, including more than thirty-three species of bees and wasps and more than twenty species of butterflies and moths.

As you leave Kennedy Forest, you may continue east along Government Drive to reach the North Entrance of the Saint Louis Zoo or take Wells Drive east to the South Entrance.

3 Saint Louis Zoo

The zoo's 1904 Flight Cage was built by the Smithsonian Institution for the World's Fair, but the city of St. Louis purchased it after the fair was over, inspiring the official founding of the Saint Louis Zoo in 1910. The zoo is home to more than seventeen thousand animals, including mammals, fish, reptiles, amphibians, birds, and arthropods (insects and arachnids, or spiders). The Saint Louis Zoo is one of only a few free zoos in the United States. The zoo's mission is to conserve animals and their habitats through animal management, research, recreation, and educational programs that encourage the support and enrich the experience of the public. Because the zoo is free, it is easy to detour from the walking tour in order to simply pop in to see a polar bear or take a gander at the gorillas.

PHOTO COURTESY OF THE MISSOURI
HISTORY MUSEUM

Once you've visited the zoo, you can take an optional walk up Art Hill to see the finest of the city's fine art. Leave from the zoo's North Entrance and take a right to walk east along Government Drive. When you come to the intersection of Fine Arts Drive, use the crosswalk to head up Fine Arts Drive toward the Saint Louis Art Museum.

WHO WERE THE FOUNDERS OF THE SAINT LOUIS ZOO?

The Saint Louis Zoo is unique in that it is "forever free" for all to visit. In 1910, the Zoological Society of St. Louis was founded, marking the beginning of the Saint Louis Zoo. The members included ornithologist Otto Widman, Professor James F. Abbott of Washington University, shirt manufacturer Cortlandt Harris, herpetologist Julius Hurter, and taxidermist Frank Schwarz. Each of these men had immigrated from Europe, where they were accustomed to zoos being a place for royalty and the upper classes to visit, making it all the more novel to create a free zoo in the United States where everyone was welcome.

PHOTO COURTESY OF THE MISSOURI HISTORY MUSEUM

❹ 1904 Flight Cage

The 1904 Flight Cage is inside the Saint Louis Zoo, but you can see it from outside the zoo's walls. To commemorate the one hundredth anniversary of the World's Fair in 2004, the zoo turned the Flight Cage into an animal habitat called Cypress Swamp, meant to mimic the Mississippi River wetlands throughout southeastern Missouri and southern Illinois. You can see twenty different species of North American birds while walking along the boardwalk inside the Cypress Swamp.

CRITTERS ALONG THE WAY

Birds

Forest Park is a dream for birders of all ages and skill levels. Even though the park is located within the city limits of St. Louis, plenty of migratory and native birds call this place home. There have been over 216 different bird species documented in Forest Park. Here is a list of just some of the birds you can look and listen for when exploring Forest Park:

Hummingbird	Killdeer	Goldfinch	Cooper's hawk
Great blue heron	Mallard duck	House finch	Northern flicker
Great egret	Wood duck	Red-winged blackbird	Mockingbird
Green heron	Barn swallow	Mourning and rock doves	Great horned owl
Black crowned night heron	Tufted titmouse	White-throated sparrow	Barred owl
Belted kingfisher	Downy woodpecker	Dark-eyed junko	Bald eagle
American kestrel	Red-bellied woodpecker	Cardinal	
Red-headed woodpecker	Carolina chickadee	Red-tailed hawk	

Insects

Depending on the season, Forest Park is home to innumerable insect species, from ladybugs and grasshoppers to beetles and walking sticks. Some consider insects to be pests, but they actually serve an important role in maintaining the ecology of the park. They provide food for animals, control plant species through their own consumption, and even serve as gardeners by pollinating trees and flowers.

Mammals

Mammals—characterized by having fur, live birth, and nursing their young—are some of the most exciting animals to spot in Forest Park. During evening or at night, you can easily see raccoons digging through trash bins for a snack or running across the roads. Opossums are another nighttime creature. Though they get a bad rap, these animals are actually North America's only marsupial. In the park's waterways, you may be able to spot a mink. These relatives of otters or weasels are semiaquatic, meaning they can be found on either land or water. Even animals as large as white-tailed deer sometimes turn up in the park. Finally, keep an eye out for the park's few resident canids, like foxes and coyotes. These adaptable animals are able to live in suburban and even urban areas, such as Forest Park.

Reptiles and Amphibians

Keep your eyes peeled for some of the smaller animal life in the park, like its resident reptiles and amphibians. Freshwater turtles can be seen in the park's waterways. Frogs and toads are an important part of Forest Park's ecosystem, keeping insect populations in check and adding their famous chorus to summer nights. And, yes, you can find snakes in Forest Park, but they are nothing to be afraid of—in fact, they help the ecosystem too by preying on rodent populations. Snakes are not aggressive unless threatened.

Tree Species

How did Forest Park get its name? It's filled with trees, of course! Forest Park is home to nearly 220 tree species. Forest Park Forever and its partners work hard to maintain over 45,000 trees within the boundaries of the park. Much of the forest land in Missouri is of the oak-hickory type, so you'll see many species of these two trees. Of course, in the spring, visitors can easily spot the beautiful blooming redbuds, dogwoods, and serviceberry trees as they display their seasonal colors. In the park's native habitats, Forest Park Forever's use of prescribed burns supports trees predating the park to naturally regenerate as a way to connect our history and our future. The park's trees not only create a pleasant environment for visitors but also make homes for native wildlife species, playing a crucial role in the ecology of the park.

PHOTO COURTESY OF
JoELLEN TOLER

PHOTO COURTESY OF
FOREST PARK FOREVER

PHOTO COURTESY OF
FOREST PARK FOREVER

PHOTO COURTESY OF
FOREST PARK FOREVER

AFTERWORD

From Forest Park's June 1876 opening through the day you are reading this, it is incredible to consider just how many memorable steps have been taken within these 1,300 acres. Toddlers and runners, brides and birders, World's Fair–goers and cultural explorers.

With *Forest Park: A Walk through History*, Carolyn Mueller has provided visitors of today and tomorrow with well-planned, thoughtful tours through some of the park's most scenic areas. Those readers with a longer relationship with Forest Park will recall just how striking it is that today's park is as vibrant and beautiful as it is. While the park had an exciting and storied first century, decades of deferred maintenance eventually saw the park slip into distressing decline in the 1970s and 1980s.

Since Forest Park Forever's founding in 1986, our nonprofit conservancy has been honored to partner with the city of St. Louis to bring the park back from the brink and to sustain it for millions of visitors—now and forever. With the support of generous donors, volunteers, and partners, the park has gone from a place where community members were hesitant to go in the evening to a place where they wanted to experience some of their best memories. This includes strolls along the Emerson Grand Basin, hikes through the forest, walks along the waterway . . . all of which, thanks to this book, you are now even better equipped to take.

As you plan your next walking tour through Forest Park, please know how much your visit means to our organization. People bring the park alive. And with each stroll you set out on—with unforgettable views of nature, architecture, and history—our team is further inspired to continue sustaining the magic of Forest Park.

We look forward to seeing you soon!

—Lesley S. Hoffarth, P.E.
President and Executive Director
Forest Park Forever

SOURCES

1. "Biography of Saint Louis IX, King of France (1214–1270)." Church of St. Louis, King of France, www.stlouiskingoffrance.org/our-church/saint-louis-ix/.

2. Corrigan, Don H., and Holly Shanks. 2017. *Forest Park*. Charleston, S.C.: Arcadia Publishing.

3. "Collection Highlights." Saint Louis Art Museum, www.slam.org/explore-the-collection/collection-highlights/.

4. "Course History." Forest Park Golf Course, 12 June 2018, www.forestparkgc.com/course-history.

5. "Explore Forest Park." Forest Park Forever, 7 April 2015, forestparkmap.org/.

6. Forest Park Statues & Monuments, www.forestparkstatues.org/.

7. "It Started in 1905: A Brief History of Sledding on Art Hill." *St. Louis Post-Dispatch*, 10 January 2019, www.stltoday.com/news/archives/it-started-in-a-brief-history-of-sledding-on-art/collection_402ee3a3-6ad0-56d2-b006-a1c370255d06.html#anchor_item_21.

8. "Jewel Box." City of St. Louis, www.stlouis-mo.gov/government/departments/parks/parks/Jewel-Box.cfm.

9. Matousek, Mark. "Q&A: Grand Basin Poses New Challenges for Water Skiers." *St. Louis Post-Dispatch*, 26 June 2014. www.stltoday.com/entertainment/q-a-grand-basin-poses-new-challenges-for-waterskiers/article_7b1cab6f-39bf-51d3-acbe-e1853a6d99a2.html."]

10. "Nature Playscape." Forest Park Forever, www.forestparkforever.org/playscape.

11. "History of the Zoo." Saint Louis Zoo, www.stlzoo.org/about/history.

12. "Mission." Saint Louis Zoo, www.stlzoo.org/about/mission.

INDEX